✓ **W9-CGK-716**

Disastrous

Earthquakes

by Henry Gilfond

Franklin Watts
New York/London/Toronto/Sydney/1981
A First Book

to John A. Pope, Jr.

Photographs courtesy of
The U.S. Department of Commerce/National Oce-
anic and Atmospheric Administration (NOAA): pp.
vi, 8 (EDS), 34 (top) (EDS), 34 (bottom), 37 (top)
(Mrs. Harry Simms, Sr.), 37 (bottom) (Joint Tsunami Research Effort); United Press International:
pp. 3, 54, 57; the American Red Cross: p. 13 (photo
by Ted Carland); the U.S. Department of the
Interior/Geological Survey: pp. 22, 27 (National
Earthquake Information Service, Golden, Colorado),
38, 50 (with NOAA), 51 (with NOAA); the New York
Public Library Picture Collection: p. 30; The Bett-
mann Archive: p. 46.

Cover photograph courtesy of Gamma, © F. Lochon

Map and diagram by Vantage Art, Inc.

Library of Congress Cataloging in Publication Data

Gilfond, Henry.
Disastrous earthquakes.

(A First book)
Includes index.
Summary: Explains what causes earthquakes,
how to predict and measure them, and
ways to prevent damage. Also describes
great quakes throughout history.
1. Earthquakes—Juvenile literature.
[1. Earthquakes] I. Title.
QE534.2.G54   551.2'2   81–4625
ISBN 0–531–04324–X   AACR2

Contents

Disastrous Earthquakes

1

Earthquake!

Yugoslavia's coastline along the Adriatic Sea is dotted with seaports, fishing villages, and summer resorts of various sizes. In the summertime, the hotels, streets, and beaches are crowded with tourists. The harbors are busy with all kinds of seacraft, from small pleasure boats and fishing boats to oceangoing liners. But on the morning of Easter Sunday, April 15, 1979, still months away from the influx of summer visitors, all was relatively quiet on the Yugoslavian strip along the Adriatic.

The shops were just beginning to get ready for the summer trade. The scores of hotels were just starting to get things in shape for the expected summer guests. A few Austrian and German visitors, on holiday early, were the only strangers in all of the resort towns.

At Bijela, one of the larger Yugoslav seaports and 30 miles (48 km) south of Dubrovnik, the biggest Yugoslav city on the Adriatic, fifteen ocean liners lay at rest in their docks. During the busy season, some 800 people work in the docks at Bijela. This Easter Sunday there were no more than 130 working on the big ships. All was comparatively still and peaceful in Bijela the morning of April 15, 1979. There was nothing at all to warn anybody in Bijela, or anywhere else along the Adriatic coast, of sudden disaster.

At exactly 7:20 A.M., a terrible rumbling shook the ground where the men of Bijela were working. Quickly, to a man, they scrambled up the sides of the boats for safety. Frozen with fear, they watched as the sea pulled back a few feet from the sand and docks and then, almost at once, send up a massive wave 7 feet (2.1 m) high, smashing onto the beach, the boats, and the docks.

Like small toy boats, the big ocean liners swayed at their anchors. Huge ten-story-high cranes snapped and fell into the sea. A 300-yard (270-m) -long pier cracked and sank out of sight. The customs house nearby split in two. So did the dock office, as the roofs of both buildings buckled and collapsed. The contents of both offices were scattered and floated off or disintegrated in the murky, brownish-gray waters of the Adriatic.

One customs office agent was killed instantly by the falling debris. He was not the only one to die in the earthquake, however. Nor was Bijela the only town to suffer the catastrophe.

At the resort town of Bar, twenty ships, mostly pleasure boats, were destroyed by the quake. The waterfront of the resort town of Zelenika disappeared completely in the waters of the Adriatic.

In the towns themselves, streets split down the middle; cars and trucks careened and settled at crazy angles. Enormous boulders, hurled down from the surrounding cliffs, crashed into store windows and broke down the walls of many shops, houses, and hotels. What had only moments before been neat little streets with neat little shops and dwelling places suddenly became acres

The Agava Hotel in the Bar region of Yugoslavia still stands, though cracked, crumbled, and sagging badly, after the devastating Easter Sunday earthquake of 1979.

of rubble. In Ulcinj, one of the more popular resort towns, entire streets disappeared under rubble.

Eighty to ninety percent of the houses in thirteen villages along the Adriatic were leveled to the ground. In Herceg Novi, an ancient citadel strong enough to have withstood the sieges of foreign armies for five hundred years just slid into the sea.

The casualties were comparatively light, considering the awesome power of the earthquake, the worst in Yugoslavia's history. Ninety-four people lost their lives and 1,200 were injured. Neighboring Albania reported 35 deaths and 330 injuries in the quake. Fortunately, the earthquake occurred in the off-season of this tourist area. Fortunate, too, that it was Sunday morning, when so many of the early-rising Yugoslavs were already out in the streets, walking, marketing, or on their way to church—instead of inside their collapsing houses. If the earthquake had occurred in midsummer, with the towns teeming with people, and after dark, the loss of life would have been much greater, counted perhaps in the thousands.

Still, 80,000 people of this Adriatic coastline lost their homes. The walls of their houses and apartment buildings had sagged and cracked. Some had fallen into the sea. Thousands whose houses had not been completely destroyed by the earthquake feared that the structures of their homes had been weakened and that living in them would be unsafe. Therefore they abandoned them and set up housekeeping, along with tens of thousands of others, among the olive groves.

A great many wished to flee from the coast to seek safety in parts of the country that had not felt the impact of the earthquake. But traveling was almost impossible. The roads they needed to take to reach a safe haven, through the rugged Yugoslav mountains, had been hit by the quake, too, and were in shambles. Army engineers worked around the clock, clearing the debris, moving boulders, dragging cars and trucks out of deep ditches, and trying to repair the huge cracks that had appeared in the bridges. The Yugoslav government estimated that the damage created by the earthquake totaled the equivalent of more than $450 million.

The earthquake in Yugoslavia was not the only major earthquake in 1979. Earlier in the year, on January 16, a quake that shook eastern Iran and western Pakistan killed hundreds of people and destroyed at least a thousand homes. All in all, there were about a million earthquakes in 1979, though most were very small. And in March 1980, an earthquake preceded by just one week, or perhaps triggered, the first small eruptions of volcanic Mount St. Helens in the state of Washington. Thirty or forty earth tremors shook the area before the major blast of the volcano on May 18 killed over sixty people, snapped trees and bridges, and buried acres of land in its mudflows.

The earth is indeed a restless and volatile planet.

Every Thirty Seconds

On an average, every thirty seconds, year in and year out, the earth trembles, rumbles, quivers, or quakes. Seismologists record the occurrence of about one million earthquakes every year. The vast majority of these quakes are so slight that only seismographs, the delicate measuring instruments of seismologists, can detect them. They are earthquakes, nevertheless.

People who work on the upper floors of huge skyscrapers sometimes will detect a slight shudder, the slightest of vibrations, in their offices. At such times, they will have experienced an earthquake, an extremely mild earthquake, but an earthquake still.

At home, sometimes, a hanging plant may suddenly begin to sway slightly for no apparent reason. There will be a feeling of vibrations in the house, as if a heavy truck were riding close by or a supersonic plane were flying overhead. At such times, the earthquake is considered by seismologists as rather slight.

What seismologists call a moderate earthquake can be recognized by anyone. It will rattle the dishes in their cupboards. The floors of the house will creak. So may the walls. A chair or a table may suddenly start to move.

A stronger quake will shake the pictures off the walls, toss dishes off their shelves, and send even heavy furniture moving across the room. Still stronger quakes will wake you from your sleep, no matter how deep. The plaster of the walls in your house will crack, even begin to fall. Dishes will rattle and crash to the floor. Chairs and tables will slide around the room. Even heavy beds will roll about in the bedrooms. This kind of earthquake is cause for considerable concern, if not alarm.

When chairs and tables and other furniture begin to turn over, and plaster falls from your ceilings, you are experiencing what is called a strong earthquake. In such an earthquake, houses and other structures that have not been built too well will suffer considerable damage, such as collapsed roofs and fallen walls. When bricks begin to loosen and fall from buildings and pieces of tile begin to crash into the streets from chimneys, you are in the midst of an even more powerful earthquake. Earthquakes of this intensity will be strong enough to overturn monuments marking the graves in cemeteries.

Thus far we have described eight kinds of earthquakes the earth experiences, classified according to strength, or intensity. As measured by the so-called Mercalli scale of earthquake intensity, there are another four, each one stronger than the previous one.

In earthquakes measuring nine on this scale, buildings will shift from their foundations. Some will collapse. There will be cracks in the ground where there were no cracks before. Underground gas pipes and water pipes may be broken.

An earthquake that registers a ten on the Mercalli scale of

An earthquake measuring an eleven in intensity will collapse bridges. This is a bridge in Niigata, Japan, that fell as a result of a June 16, 1964 earthquake.

intensity will destroy a great number of buildings, whether they are built of stone, brick, or wood. It will bend railroad tracks. It will create landslides. It will do considerable damage to underground pipes.

An earthquake that measures an eleven in intensity will destroy every structure except those buildings that have been constructed of reinforced concrete, or those that have steel-skeleton construction. Debris will bury the broken streets. Bridges will collapse. Underground pipes will all be broken. There will be no electricity in your city or town, no gas, and no water. This kind of earthquake will create an almost complete disaster.

The maximum damage is done by an earthquake that measures a twelve in intensity. In such an earthquake there is total damage, catastrophe.

If you live in Los Angeles or San Francisco, you have probably experienced earthquakes of minor intensity any number of times. You have probably become quite accustomed to the slighter kinds of tremors, the small vibrations that pass in seconds, the rattling of dishes, and the slight swaying of the ground on which you walk. "I think that was an earthquake," you most likely say, and immediately forget all about it.

Such slight quakes are common in Los Angeles and San Francisco and never make the newspapers. The vast majority of earthquakes, as we have already indicated, are like this, and no mention of them is made in the press or on television or radio.

Earthquakes of even medium intensity, however, are sure to make the newspapers and the airwaves. It was such an earthquake that jolted the southern coast of California on New Year's Day of 1979. The earthquake itself did not cause too much damage, but it was strong enough to create landslides along the bluffs overlooking the Pacific Coast Highway in Malibu. Another medium-intensity quake jolted all of southern California a little more than two weeks later, on January 16, 1979.

A mild earthquake surprised the state of New Jersey and parts of Brooklyn and Staten Island in New York City on January 30, 1979. The quake did very little damage. It was only the unexpected appearance of it, in an area that is generally free of earthquakes, that made it newsworthy.

On the twenty-second of February of that same year, Mexico City experienced a relatively mild quake. On the twenty-eighth, it experienced three mild tremors. But on that same day, an earthquake struck a wide area of the Yukon territory in Canada. Fortunately, little damage and no casualties were reported from the Yukon and Mexico City. However, just two weeks later, on March 14, a more powerful earthquake struck a vast area of Mexico, killing at least one person and injuring twenty-one.

There was an earthquake that jolted much of Colombia in South America on the eleventh of March, 1979. Athens, Greece, suffered an earthquake of medium intensity just two days later. Neither of these earthquakes was of the intensity of those that hit Yugoslavia and Iran that same year, but medium earthquakes are not uncommon, particularly along the earth's two earthquake "belts," or "corridors."

One of these corridors runs along the borders of the land masses that ring the Pacific Ocean, on both the Asian and American sides of the globe, with branches that extend into the West Indies and the Southern Antilles. Alaska and California lie in this corridor. The San Andreas fault system, along which most earthquakes in North America have occurred, runs for about 700 miles (1,120 km) from northern California down to the Mexican border.

The other earthquake corridor runs through the East Indies; the Himalaya Mountains; Hindu Kush in Afghanistan; Iran; the Caucasus Mountains; Turkey; the Carpathian Moun-

Earthquake
Corridors

Greenland

North
American

Ring of
Fire

South
America

Ring of
Fire

China

Europe

Arabia

Africa

Australia

tains in Czechoslovakia, Hungary, the Soviet Union, and Rumania; the Apennines that form the spine of all Italy; the Alps from France to Albania; and the Atlas Mountains in northwest Africa.

Earthquakes have occurred and continue to occur in many other parts of the world. Washington, D.C., has suffered some fifteen earthquakes in the last 245 years but no real damage. New York experienced eight or nine earthquakes during this same period. Its worst quake was on August 10, 1884, and that did little more than damage a few houses in the vicinity of Jamaica and Amityville.

London, England, has experienced a great many more quakes, at least 1,500, but its severest earthquake came in 1884 also. The quake lasted for only ten seconds. That was long enough, though, to topple hundreds of chimneys and otherwise damage hundreds of houses, as well as break up numerous streets and set the water rising in many wells.

Actually, though, almost 99 percent of the world's earthquakes occur along the two earthquake corridors, especially the most severe earthquakes.

Of the average million or more earthquakes each year, about twenty will be strong enough to create serious or extensive damage. About two on an average, though sometimes as many as five, of these earthquakes are devastating or catastrophic in their effects, resulting in death and widespread destruction.

The last catastrophic earthquake in the Western Hemisphere occurred on February 4, 1976, in Guatemala. More than 23,000 men, women, and children lost their lives in that quake.

More than 23,000 people lost their lives in the catastrophic Guatemalan earthquake of February 4, 1976.

The last major earthquake to hit the United States occurred on February 9, 1971, in California's San Fernando Valley. Sixty-two people were killed immediately by the catastrophe, and property damage came to over one billion dollars.

But it is not always the earthquakes of greatest intensity that create the most damage or kill the most people. In 1960, an earthquake that was only moderate in intensity killed 700 men, women, and children in Lar, Iran, and injured thousands more. A similarly moderate earthquake that same year killed 10,000 to 12,000 in Agadir, Morocco. In both cities, living conditions are crowded and most of the structures are flimsy. Comparatively minor earthquakes can wreak havoc in such areas.

3

Earthquakes and Myth

In ancient times, people generally believed that the gods were responsible for every natural phenomenon, including rain, thunder, lightning, drought, floods, volcanic eruptions, and earthquakes. There were a few cultures, however, that believed it was some unnaturally large creature that caused earthquakes.

The ancient Japanese, for example, at one time were certain that earthquakes were caused by a great spider living under the earth and moving around in its dwelling place. Later, the ancient Japanese attributed earthquakes to the movement of a giant underground catfish.

In Mongolia and the Celebes, it was believed that a giant underground hog was responsible for earthquakes. In parts of South America, the people believed it was a whale under the earth that created the quakes. North American Indians said it was a giant tortoise that made the earth tremble and shake.

In Siberia, the people of Kamchatka said that it was the

dogs belonging to the god Tuil who caused the earth tremors. The dogs were infested with fleas, they said. Occasionally, while being walked by Tuil, the dogs stopped to scratch. It was this scratching, they believed, that disturbed the earth and caused the upheavals.

The ancient Greek philosopher Aristotle was one of the first to offer a scientific explanation of earthquakes. He believed that there were great winds that blew under the surface of the earth. When the winds became bottled up in a particular underground area and had nowhere else to move, they erupted through the crust of the earth. The trembling, the rumbling, and the quake with all of its destruction were the result of this breakthrough.

Aristotle's theory was generally accepted as the true explanation for the cause of earthquakes even in the times of Shakespeare. In one Shakespearean play, a leading character speaks of nature "breaking forth in strange eruptions." Imprisoned wind shakes the earth and "topples down steeples and moss-grown towers."

Others around this time, seeking a better explanation for the cause of earthquakes, suggested that earthquakes came about when huge underground caverns collapsed, shaking the ground above in the process.

Neither the theory of Aristotle nor the other was correct. As we shall see later in this book, over the years we have greatly increased our understanding of earthquakes. However, the exact cause of earthquakes remains a mystery.

Curiously, certain age-old myths concerning earthquakes still persist.

Some people still believe, for example, as they did in ancient times, that the air is unnaturally quiet before an earthquake. Others have said that animals become particularly restless and alarmed before the onslaught of a quake. Actually, there is strong evidence for this theory. The Chinese have reported pigs rooting at their fences, cows breaking their halters to escape, rats behaving as though they were drunk, chickens refusing to enter their coops, birds crying in an agitated manner, and more, all before an impending earthquake. However, just how these animals sense the coming of an earthquake has yet to be discovered.

There have been many strange tales about earthquakes, especially of the earth opening up during a quake to swallow people, houses, even whole villages, then closing up again and burying everything alive, leaving not a trace of the life that had lived on the land before the quake.

No one has ever been able to verify such an incident. Once, people were summoned to come quickly to see where the earth had opened and then closed, leaving only the tail of a cow above ground. When the people reached the scene, the cow's tail had disappeared. The explanation given at the time was that dogs had eaten it.

Many such stories have been told and believed through the centuries of millions of earthquakes.

Other phenomena said to occur during an earthquake are great flashes of fire erupting from the earth itself during the quake. There has been no scientific evidence of such fires. But electrical short circuits, thunderstorms, even meteor swarms in the skies—any or all of which may occur during a violent earthquake—may easily be mistaken for flashes of fire erupting from the bowels of the earth.

Perhaps the most interesting story in the history of earthquakes concerns the lost continent of Atlantis.

The ancient Greek philosopher Plato spoke of Atlantis as an island in the Atlantic Ocean, west of Gibraltar, that sank under the sea. The ancient Egyptians were the first to mention it, telling the ancient Athenians that a large island off Greece had disappeared, been swallowed up by the sea overnight, and that only a handful of small islands were all that remained of a great continent.

For many years people pondered over this lost island and some wrote fanciful tales about it. But the latest thinking, based on actual exploration and careful scientific research, seems to bring us closer to the truth of that fabulous "continent."

First, Atlantis was an island, and it was in the waters off Greece. Second, it did disappear overnight in those waters almost completely, as the ancient Egyptians had reported. On those points, at least, the legends were accurate.

But marine geologists delved deeply into the seabed off Greece. Archeologists dug in the ruins of the remaining small islands in the area. The conclusion they came to is that Thera, one of the small islands, and its neighbors constituted the "lost continent" of Atlantis and that a huge earthquake followed by a mighty volcanic eruption buried underwater the greater part of the land. Volcanic eruptions often follow earthquakes, as earthquakes will often follow volcanic eruptions. In this case, the dual upheavals of nature destroyed not only "Atlantis" but also the famous Minoan culture of Crete. It was one of the mightiest and most dramatic of such upheavals in history.

4

Stress, Strain, and Quake

Minor earthquakes are sometimes caused by the movement of liquid rock, underground, in volcanoes. Such an earthquake may occur because of collapsing underground spaces between extinct volcanoes, that is, volcanoes that are dead. Sometimes a particularly heavy landslide will create a minor quake. In all these instances, the crust of the earth is disturbed, and the earth will tremble in reaction to the disturbance. Earthquakes stemming from these causes are generally limited in their intensities, but, as noted before, they can create a great deal of damage depending on where they occur.

It is the tectonic earthquake that generally causes catastrophe. A tectonic earthquake is a quake that results from movement in the earth's crust, its outer shell. This crust is about 40 miles (64 km) thick. It consists almost entirely of cool rock, rigid in normal circumstances.

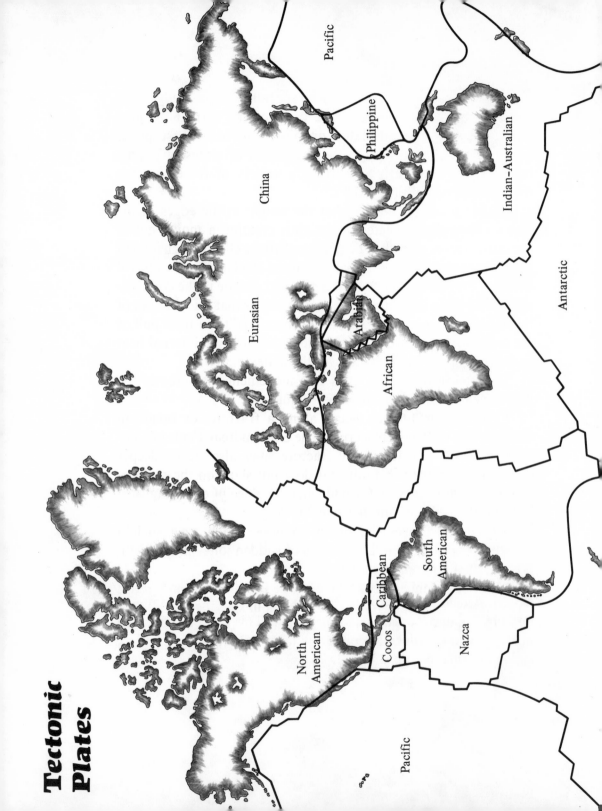

Tectonic
Plates

Pacific

Philippine

China

Indian–Australian

Eurasian

Arabian

African

Antarctic

South
American

Caribbean

North
American

Cocos

Nazca

Pacific

The majority of geologists who specialize in the study of the earth's structure believe that the crust of the earth is divided into a number of small plates, or masses of rock. These plates usually fit together closely, like the pieces of a jigsaw puzzle, but they are constantly moved by a variety of forces coming from the interior of the earth.

Some scientists believe that the weight at the edges of the plates may pull the plates down, thus creating a movement in the crust. Other scientists believe that it is a chemical change in the plate that creates an imbalance in its structure and causes it to move. Still others believe it is a physical change in the composition of the plate that causes the movement or that it is the spin of the earth around its axis. And still others credit the tidal pull of the moon for the movement or believe that it is the internal heat at the core of the earth that moves the plates.

Whatever the cause, it is this movement that creates the tectonic earthquake, the major earthquake.

The movement may occur along a fracture, or break, in the structure of the earth's crust. The San Andreas Fault in California is such a fracture. A fracture may also occur deeper down in the earth, in a fault that does not show on the surface. (Such a fracture may be formed when the edge of one plate slips over onto the edge of another plate.)

Whatever causes the plates to move, each time such a movement occurs, there are a series of sudden jolts on the earth. We call these jolts *earthquakes*.

The place under the surface of the earth where such a jolt takes place is called the *focus* of the earthquake.

The section of the earth directly above the focus is called the *epicenter* of the earthquake. It is at the epicenter that the earthquake creates its greatest damage.

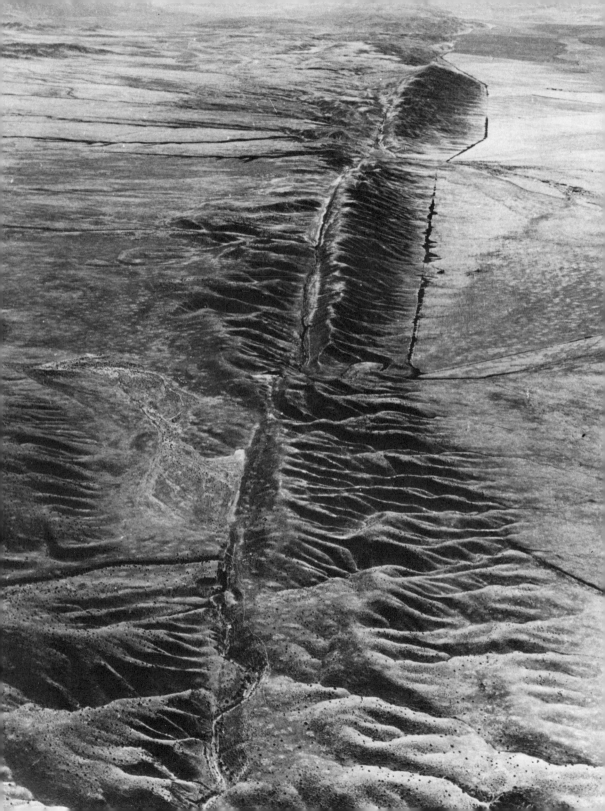

The epicenter very often will suffer what are called *after-shocks*, quakes that come soon after the first major quake has shaken the area. Mexico, as already noted, suffered five earth tremors in 1979, all within a space of seven days. There are times when an earthquake's aftershocks will last for more than a year. Evidently, it often takes time for the "plates" to settle down and become quiet after one of their movements.

Nor does the epicenter alone suffer from this movement of the plates and the earthquakes that result. We have already noted that the Yugoslav earthquake of 1979 affected not only a 200-mile (320-km) stretch of the Adriatic coastline but also the neighboring country of Albania. The earthquake that hit the Yukon Territory in Canada hit a wide area of Alaska on the very same day.

When the movement of a plate jars the earth, it sends out waves. These waves travel through the earth at a rate of 2 to 5 miles (3.2 to 8 km) a second. Their effects may be felt many miles from the epicenter of the earthquake. An earthquake that occurred on March 29, 1954, in Granada, Spain, sent shocks as far away as Algiers in Africa.

When Lisbon, Portugal, was the epicenter of a mighty earthquake in 1755, shocks were felt as far as 1,400 miles (2,240 km) away. All of Portugal and Spain were violently shaken by the quake. So were the south of France and North Africa. Italy, Switzerland, Scotland, Ireland, the Scandinavian countries, Holland, and Germany all felt tremors. When Assam, in the northeast corner of India, was hit by an earthquake on June 12, 1897,

The San Andreas Fault in the
Carrizo Plain area of California

the cathedral and town hall of Calcutta, 550 miles (880 km) from the epicenter of the quake, were heavily damaged, and any number of houses were completely destroyed. Over an area of 10,000 square miles (26,000 sq km) every building made of brick or stone was leveled to the ground. Another area of about 150,000 square miles (390,000 sq km) experienced the tremors that come with a more powerful earthquake. An area of more than 1,950,000 square miles (5,070,000 sq km)—about half the size of the entire continent of Europe—felt the shock of the quake at Assam.

The earthquakes in Lisbon and Assam were particularly strong, but the earth has suffered many such quakes over the centuries, quakes that rock great sections of the globe, hurling huge boulders into the air; creating massive landslides; burying islands under the sea; leveling houses, churches, whole villages and towns; and killing and maiming thousands of people. But as we have already noted, earthquakes of even medium or slight intensity also may send out great waves of destruction.

On August 15, 1950, an earthquake with its epicenter some 300 miles (480 km) northeast of Assam destroyed that city again and wreaked havoc in India, Burma, Pakistan, mountainous Tibet, and China.

But even earthquakes whose waves of destruction are more limited, as they were in the Chinese earthquake of 1976, can kill as many as 250,000 people.

Waves generated by earthquakes, it might be noted, have their strongest effect in areas where there are fractures or faults in the earth. The strongest of these waves can crack the earth's crust, from deep down all the way to the surface of the earth. These are the waves that destroy whole cities and all the people who live in them.

5

Measuring Earthquakes

Earthquakes can be measured for intensity, magnitude, or both.

The measurement of an earthquake's intensity informs us of the quake's effect on the surface of the earth—the cracks in the ground, the landslides, the upheaval of waters, the damage to buildings of all kinds, the number of people killed, the number of injured, and so on.

The most commonly used scale for this kind of measurement was developed by the Italian seismologist, Giuseppi Mercalli, back in 1902. The Mercalli scale was later modified by American seismologists Harry O. Wood and Frank Neumann, among others. There are twelve intensities defined by the Mercalli scale, ranging from the slightest earthquake that can be detected only by a very sensitive seismograph to an earthquake that leaves utter destruction in its wake.

Actually, anyone at the site of an earthquake can esti-
mate without any scientific instruments the intensity of all but
the very slightest quake. The different grades in the scale are
listed and described in Chapter 2 of this book.

The intensity of an earthquake is not, however, the same
in every area that is affected by the quake. In each case and for
each location that experiences the earthquake, the intensity will
depend upon several factors. First, the intensity of the quake will
almost always be strongest at its epicenter. The farther away an
area is from the epicenter, the more likely it is that there will be
a weakening of the intensity.

This is not *always* true. It depends to a great extent on the
nature of the ground and the solidity of the buildings at both
the epicenter and away from it. The epicenter of an earthquake
may be far out at sea, and this is not an uncommon occurrence.
The intensity of such an earthquake at its epicenter might be
practically nonexistent; but its shock waves, reaching land, might
create havoc. An eruption in the Atlantic Ocean, for example, in
May 1958, was responsible for hundreds of shocks in Fayal, an
island in the Azores. The shocks destroyed more than a thousand
houses on the island and devastated a great number of its
villages, all in one disastrous night.

Where buildings are well constructed, a quake is likely to
do less damage, and therefore its intensity would be considered
low. On the other hand, where buildings are of flimsy construction, the damage and the loss of life will be greater, and the intensity of the earthquake in this case would be considered high
on the Mercalli scale.

The second way earthquakes are measured is by their magnitude, the term given to the amount of energy the quake releases at its source, its focus. This magnitude, unlike the intensity of an earthquake, does not vary from place to place. An

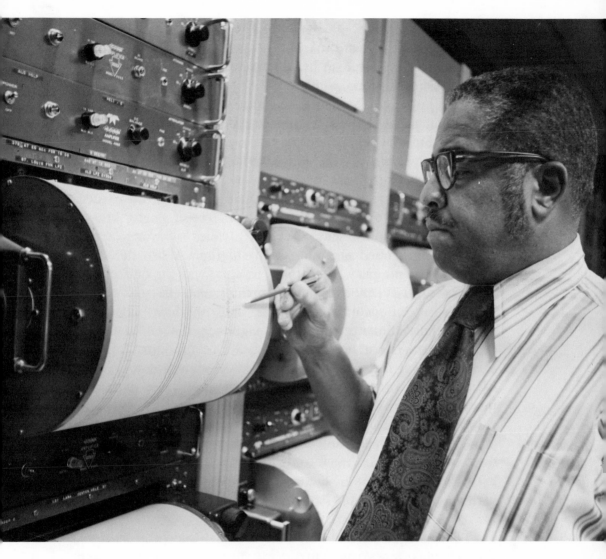

*Geophysicist Waverly J. Person points
to an earthquake seismograph recording
that triggered an earthquake alarm.*

earthquake has only one magnitude, which can be measured only by scientific instruments, not by observation of the effects of the quake. The instrument for measuring an earthquake's magnitude is called a *seismograph*.

The seismograph scale begins at zero. At zero, the seismograph indicates a very slight, almost undetectable earth tremor, certainly a tremor that cannot be felt even by someone standing right on the epicenter of the quake.

From zero, the scale moves up by ones, but each whole number indicates a multiple of ten; that is, when a magnitude of 1 is indicated on the seismograph, the seismologist knows that the magnitude of the quake is ten times as strong as the quake that measured zero on the seismograph. When the scale measures 3, the quake is ten times as strong as the quake that measured 2 and a thousand times greater than the zero earthquake. A magnitude of 7 is ten times as strong as a magnitude of 6, a hundred times as strong as a magnitude of 5, ten thousand times as strong as a magnitude of 3, and ten million times as strong as a magnitude of zero. In other words, each increase of a whole number of the scale represents a tenfold increase in the magnitude of the earthquake.

Few earthquakes have reached a magnitude of 9 in the years since the seismograph was invented (see later in this chapter), but many have come close to it. Among them were the earthquake in Sanriku, Japan, on March 3, 1933, and the earthquake in Chile that killed between 5,000 and 10,000 people on May 22, 1960.

The earthquake that killed more than 1,500 people in Assam on August 15, 1950, had a magnitude of 8.7. The quake that killed 82,000 people in Messina, Italy, on December 28, 1908, had a magnitude of 7.5. The great San Francisco earthquake of April 18, 1906, had a magnitude of 8.3.

Generally, when the magnitude of an earthquake measures as much as 7, it becomes necessary to evacuate the area close to the epicenter of the quake. A quake that measures 8 or more on the seismograph promises utter disaster in the area of the epicenter. There have been about forty earthquakes with a magnitude of 8 or more since the end of the nineteenth century.

The efforts on the part of scientists to measure the strength of earthquakes goes back a long time in history. The first person to develop an instrument for such purpose, as far as we have been able to learn, was a Chinese astronomer and geographer named Chang Heng.

It was in A.D. 132 that Chang developed what he called his "earthquake weathercock." This instrument, made of fine cast bronze, was made in the shape of a wine jar. Its diameter was about 3 feet (0.9 m), and it was 8 feet (2.4 m) tall. It had a dome cover, and its surface was decorated with designs of mountains, birds, tortoises, and other animals. Eight dragon heads were set on the outside of the vessel. Each dragon held a bronze ball in its mouth. Around the base of the vessel were eight bronze toads.

The operation of Chang Heng's invention was quite simple. When an earthquake occurred and sent its waves moving through the earth, Chang's vessel would vibrate with the movement of the earth. If the vibrations were strong enough, they would cause a bronze ball to fall from a dragon's mouth into the mouth of the toad below. The falling ball would indicate not only the occurrence of an earthquake but also the direction from which the shock wave came.

There is no doubt that the "earthquake weathercock" was a very clever invention. It was certainly limited, however, in its ability to measure the intensity and magnitude of earthquakes.

Nevertheless, there was no change in the device for almost

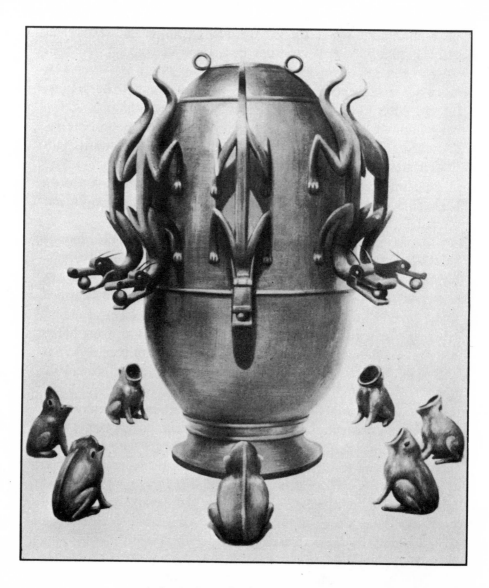

A depiction of Chang's "earthquake weathercock"

1,600 years. It was not until the beginning of the eighteenth century that a French scientist, Paul Gabriel Hautefeuille, improved on the Chinese "weathercock."

Chang had attached an ingenious dragon-bell to his invention. The bell would ring to let him know that one of the bronze balls had fallen into a toad's mouth. De Hautefeuille removed the dragon-bell and substituted a bowl of mercury. The bowl was equipped with spouts all around its rim. An earthquake shock would spill the mercury, and by measuring the amount of mercury spilled it was possible to gauge the intensity of the earthquake shock.

In 1853, Luigi Palmieri, the director of the Vulcanological Observatory in Vesuvius, Italy, invented a clock instrument that stopped at the beginning of an earthquake shock and set a recording drum in motion to see just how long the shock lasted.

In 1897, John Milne, an Englishman, developed the first modern seismograph. The instrument measured the movements of the earth by recording them on a revolving drum of paper.

Milne's seismograph was refined by a number of scientists, including Charles F. Richter of the California Institute of Technology. Work on further refining the instrument continues, but for the great majority of seismologists, magnitudes of earthquakes are measured by the "Richter scale."

It is interesting to note that seismographs are also used to detect underground testing of atomic and hydrogen bombs. This is one way the United States, for example, keeps a watch on the development of Soviet nuclear weapons.

6

Elements
of Destruction

The earthquake that shook the Gulf of Corinth in 373 B.C. sank a stretch of land several miles long and almost a mile and a half (2.4 km) wide beneath the sea. The 1923 earthquake in Japan moved whole areas of land in an east-south-easterly direction. It moved the entire island of Ooshima 13 feet (3.9 m) toward the north. In Anchorage, Alaska, the earthquake of 1964 dropped buildings and pavements as much as 30 feet (9 m); in Kodiak Island and the Kenai Peninsula, the land sank as much as 8 feet (2.4 m).

But earthquakes do not only sink land; they also raise it. During that same earthquake in Alaska, Prince William Sound rose, in certain places, as much as 33 feet (9.9 m). During the many violent earthquakes that took place along the Mississippi River between Memphis and St. Louis from December 16, 1811, to February 8, 1812, parts of the area were raised by as much as 20 feet (6 m). There are marshes, ponds, and lakes on this raised land today. One of those lakes is the St. Francis, 37 miles (59 km) long and 1.5 miles (2.4 km) wide.

Fortunately, that region of the Mississippi was sparsely populated at the time of those earthquakes; otherwise the casualties would have been enormous. Upheavals that accompany earthquakes of great magnitude almost always prove to be catastrophic. The catastrophies are created not only by the shocks of the quake but also by the landslides, fires, and tidal waves that often develop with the tremors.

In the 1783 earthquake in Calabria, Italy, acres of land were moved fully half a mile (0.8 km) across a ravine. Fifty thousand people lost their lives in that earthquake.

In the 1923 earthquake in Japan, the forest preserves of Mount Hakone and Mount Tanzawa slid into the waters. In one of the many landslides that accompanied the quake, rocks and debris plunged down a mountain valley at the speed of 60 miles (96 km) an hour, completely wiping out a village and destroying an entire railroad line. Landslides swept houses, bridges, and a train carrying 200 passengers into the Sagami Bay. Over 143,000 people were killed by that quake, and countless thousands were severely injured.

The landslides that came with the 1957 earthquake in Iran blocked up rivers and roadways, killed 400 people, and injured thousands more.

These landslides, incidentally, blocking rivers and destroying roads, railroads, and airports, make it difficult and sometimes impossible to deliver food and much-needed medical supplies and other assistance to earthquake victims.

But landslides are not the only events that make earthquakes more disastrous than they already are. Often enough, there are great waves that come with earthquakes of great magnitude. Erroneously called tidal waves, these waves are properly

called, from the Japanese word, *tsunamis*. The wave comes in from the water at such great height and with such great strength, that it sweeps away and destroys anything and everything in its path.

We have already described the force and effect of a tsunami, as one such wave hit at Bijela during the Yugoslav earthquake of 1979. The tsunami that struck the coast of Chile during its great earthquake of 1960 made rubble of scores of towns. Hundreds of wooden houses were smashed completely, some carried by the waves as far as 6,000 feet (1,800 m) inland before they were reduced to a mass of broken timber. There they mingled with countless trees that had been uprooted from the ground and boats that lay smashed with them.

The tsunami that killed thousands of people in the great earthquake that shook Lisbon, Portugal, in 1755, was responsible, too, for the drowning of thousands of others across the Mediterranean Sea, on the coast of Morocco.

A tsunami with waves as high as 75 feet (22.5 m) destroyed houses, villages, and entire populations in the Japanese earthquake at Sanriku in 1933. In 1957, during the earthquake that struck the Aleutian Islands in the North Pacific Ocean, the

Broken streets (top) *and damage from landslides* (bottom) *are two elements of earthquake destruction. The photograph on top is of a bridge entrance near Huarmey, Peru, after a May 31, 1970 earthquake. The other photograph is of the Turnagain area in Alaska following the March 27, 1964 quake.*

tsunami hit the coasts of both the Hawaiian Islands and Hokkaido in Japan, causing extensive damage.

Tsunamis have reached heights of more than 200 feet (60 m). A tsunami with a height of 210 feet (63 m) was reported to have hit Cape Lopatka at the southern tip of Kamchatka, Siberia, during the earthquake of 1737. The greatest tsunami on record is one that swept into Gilbert Bay in the Pacific on July 9, 1958. It raced in at the speed of 100 miles (160 km) an hour, pushed a wave of water 1,740 feet (522 m) high over the opposite end of the inlet, snapped off trees as thick as 4 feet (1.2 m) in diameter, and destroyed 4 square miles (10.4 sq km) of forest reaching as far inland as 3,600 feet (1,080 m).

There is no defense whatsoever against the strength and onslaught of a wave created by an earthquake. There is not much that can be done either about the great fires that often accompany earthquakes of considerable magnitude.

During such earthquakes, water lines and gas mains are broken. Drums of kerosene and gasoline are overturned, releasing the highly flammable liquids. Stoves are overturned, igniting anything with which they come into contact. The gas released from their pipes and the spilled kerosene and gasoline all feed the flames. Rooms begin to burn. Houses begin to burn. The fires spread.

Initially, the small fires can be extinguished. But the shocks of the earthquake can create a panic, even among normally

These photographs of a beachfront in Hawaii were taken right before the onslaught of a tsunami generated by an earthquake. The inhabitants of the island flee in terror.

−36

San Francisco, crumbled by an earthquake
on April 18, 1906, burns to the ground.

calm people. In their haste to get into the streets and out of their homes, which are threatening to collapse around them, people are not inclined to be concerned about the small fire that may have started to burn in their kitchens, bedrooms, or living rooms. They won't stop to pull the plugs out of their electric sockets or cut off their home's supply of electric current. It is these small fires that become, in so many cases, a great conflagration and destroy not only houses but whole towns and cities.

It was fire in the great San Francisco earthquake of 1906 that was largely responsible for the $20 million in property damage and the estimated 700 deaths that occurred during the earthquake. For three days, those who were spared their lives watched from the hills surrounding San Francisco as the fires raged, utterly destroying the city.

Tokyo was almost 50 miles (80 km) away from the epicenter of the great earthquake that shook Japan on September 1, 1923. It was a victim of the quake's shocks, nevertheless, and of the fire that came with them. More than two hundred fires broke out in the city at the same time, and 65 percent of Tokyo was gutted by the flames. Yokohama was burned to the ground. Ninety-five percent of the property lost in both cities during and following the quake was due to fire. Two-thirds of the 150,000 people killed and the more than 100,000 injured were victims not of the quake, but of fires.

Sometimes lightning from electric storms will feed such a fire, striking a house or trees in the area of the quake. High winds will feed the flames and spread the fire. If the earthquake shocks have been severe, all water lines will have been broken, and there will be nothing with which to fight the fires, even after the shocks of the earthquake have stopped.

The fires eventually will burn themselves out, but not, in most cases, before they have destroyed everything the earthquake itself has not.

7

To Prevent Damage

The best way to prevent property damage or loss of life in an earthquake is to live and work in an area that is not highly vulnerable to earth tremors. This may be rather difficult if not impossible to do, if your home lies somewhere on or near the earthquake belts that circle the globe. Californians and Japanese, Italians along the Apennines, and the people of the East Indies, among others, cannot escape the possibility that an earthquake may strike at any time in the region that is their home.

People in these regions, however, can do something about the structures in which they live and can work to minimize the possible destruction of an earthquake. Architects and engineers are well aware of the principles involved in constructing earthquake-resistant, if not earthquake-proof, structures.

First, for greatest earthquake resistance, the foundations of a building must be set on solid rock. Foundations on glacial till, which is a mixture of clay, sand, gravel, and boulders, will prove almost as earthquake-resistant as solid rock. Buildings

—40

constructed on sand and gravel or on the sediment built up by rivers will not hold up too well in earthquakes. The shocks of an earthquake are three to ten times more likely to damage structures erected on "made land," or landfills.

Thick or heavy walls do not increase resistance to earthquake shocks. On the contrary, because they are generally not made strong in spite of their being thick, they cannot resist the stresses of the shocks, and the walls crack, causing the building to come tumbling down and killing all of its occupants.

Unless they are especially well built, brick buildings also will frequently come apart in an earthquake. Tiled roofs have no place in earthquake country. Tiles come crashing down from roofs even during moderate earth tremors, and the danger of falling tile to people in the streets is considerable.

The main thing to be done in the building of an earthquake-resistant structure is to tie all parts of the structure together so that it becomes a single unit. The walls, joints, floors, and supporting columns must be joined so that, in case of a quake, the entire building vibrates as an entity. Each part of the structure supports the others, and there is no one part that will suffer more stress than another.

Modern skyscrapers are built in this fashion. They will sway in strong winds and earth tremors but remain undamaged. A number of ancient cathedrals have stood unharmed in earthquakes because their flying buttresses helped the walls of the structure to withstand abnormal stresses brought on by quakes.

The Imperial Hotel in Tokyo, designed by the noted American architect Frank Lloyd Wright, was built specifically as an earthquake-resistant structure. It stood up, unharmed, during the 1923 earthquake that ravaged the whole city. Wright also had the foresight to have a large ornamental pool constructed for the hotel. It was the water in the pool that saved the Imperial Hotel from the fires that almost destroyed the entire city. There was no other water available in Tokyo. The earthquake had torn up all the city's water mains.

Earthquake-resistant buildings cost more to construct, perhaps 10 percent more than non-resistant buildings. But the cost is negligible compared with the amount of damage an earthquake can wreak on weaker structures.

Of course, no architect or engineer can yet construct a building that will withstand the thrust of an earthquake at its epicenter. In such a case, the structure, however well made, will be torn up from the ground and smashed completely.

What can you do, personally, to protect yourself in an earthquake? First, turn off all the electric switches in your home. This should help prevent electrical fires in the walls of the building. Second, lie under some piece of furniture—a bed, a heavy table, etc.—that can protect you from falling plaster, wood, brick, or stone. Count off seconds until you have reached a minute. Generally, the tremors of an earthquake do not last much longer than a minute. Then go out into the street, away from the sides of buildings. Sometimes a weakened building will take a little time before it begins to crumble and come down.

If you feel that the house or other structure you are in is safer than the street, stand in a doorway between two rooms or in a corner of a room. These are generally the spots that can take the most stress.

If the outside walls of the building collapse, do not panic. Wait till the rubble stops falling before you move out of the structure. Then get to some wide-open space, where you will be comparatively safe in case the earthquake's aftershocks create more damage.

Of course you can do nothing in the event of a landslide or a tsunami. In the Lisbon quake of 1755, most of the people killed lost their lives due not to falling structures but to a tsunami that rolled into the open space to which they had fled.

8

Great Earthquakes in Antiquity

Between the years A.D. 10 and A.D. 1700, there were at least 3,000 major earthquakes, according to students and historians of this restless planet. There were major earthquakes before the birth of Christ, too. Undoubtedly, earthquakes have been shattering and changing the surface of the earth since the beginning of time on this globe.

The earliest of these quakes are known only by legend, stories that have come down to us by word of mouth. The oldest of these legends is about the lost island of Atlantis. This is the island that, overnight, is said to have disappeared under the sea in an earthquake that occurred some twelve thousand years ago, ten thousand years before Christ. Recently discovered scientific evidence, particularly, leaves little doubt as to the truth in the legend, first told by ancient Egyptians to the Greeks.

According to legend, too, there was another great earthquake in the area of the ancient Greek world sometime between

-43

3000 B.C. and 2500 B.C. This quake shook the known world from the western peninsula of Asia to the Pillar of Hercules (the southern tip of Spain and Gibraltar) and from Thrace in the Balkan peninsula to Egypt.

Ancient Greek historians wrote of a series of earthquakes that shook all of Greece in the year 476 B.C. Whole towns were swallowed up by the sea. An entire peninsula disappeared almost completely under the waters; only the island of Atlanta remained.

It was during these earthquakes that the Peloponnesian armies, moving to attack Boeotia, a peninsula between the Gulf of Corinth and the Straits of Euboea, turned back and went home. For these ancient Spartans, the earthquakes were understood to be a warning from the gods. Ironically, Boeotia was saved from attack, if only temporarily, by a natural disaster.

About a hundred years later, according to the ancient Greek historians, in 373 B.C., another great earthquake hit the southern coast of the Gulf of Corinth and, again, whole stretches of land were buried under the sea, including the thriving city of Helike.

We now know that it was an earthquake that brought on the eruption of Mount Vesuvius in Italy, in the year A.D. 79. This was the eruption that buried the cities of Pompeii and Herculaneum under massive mudflows and volcanic ash, killing thousands of inhabitants.

Sixty-two years before Vesuvius, in A.D. 17, earthquakes completely destroyed thirteen towns in Asia Minor. In the year A.D. 342, about 40,000 people lost their lives in earthquakes that hit Antioch, the ancient capital of Syria, on the Orontes River. Some twelve hundred years later, in 1565, earthquakes took the lives of another 30,000 people of Antioch.

Istanbul, the capital of Turkey, has suffered more than a

dozen devastating earthquakes in the past 2,000 years. In the year 1201, hundreds of thousands of men, women, and children were killed in earthquakes that struck all the Near Eastern countries.

The most deadly earthquakes experienced in antiquity, however, occurred in a more distant part of the globe. On January 24, 1556, an earthquake that shook the heavily populated area of Shensi Province in China was responsible for the deaths of 830,000 people.

There are few details known about that devastating earthquake in China. We know more of the earthquake that struck Lisbon, Portugal, in 1755, the earthquake that was the most violent of quakes suffered in recorded history.

It was November 1, Allhallows Day, in 1755. The churches of Lisbon were crowded with worshippers. At precisely 9:40 in the morning, the ground trembled. There was a mighty rumbling, then a violent shuddering and shaking of the earth. Foundations of houses, palaces, and churches were uprooted. The whole city collapsed almost at once, and thousands of men, women, and children were instantly killed by the falling debris or buried under tons of rubble.

Those who could, ran out of the buildings into the open, and thousands sought safety on the quays of the port city. But there was safety nowhere in Lisbon that Allhallows morning. The earthquake set off a huge tsunami, and waves 20 feet (6 m) high rushed onto the shore, swallowing up the quays and drowning the thousands of people who had sought shelter on them.

Perhaps as many as 20,000 men, women, and children died in that terrible earthquake. Shocks were felt as far as 1,400 miles (2,240 km) away. Violent tremors were experienced in Spain, France, and North Africa. Water in the lakes, bays, and rivers of Italy, Switzerland, Norway, Denmark, Holland, Scot-

The earthquake at Lisbon on Allhallows Day in 1755

land, and even Germany became turbulent. A tsunami drowned thousands of people on the coast of Morocco, in Africa. At Madeira, an archipelago in the Atlantic Ocean, the sea rose about 50 feet (15 m) above its normal level. Ships broke from their moorings in Dartmouth on the English Channel and at the Dutch ports of Rotterdam and Amsterdam.

The first earthquake shock in Lisbon, at 9:40 in the morning, was followed by another one at 10:00 in the morning, and a third one at noon. The fires in the city, which had begun with the first shock, smoldered and then burst into raging flames by midday. The entire city became a giant heap of burning rubble. The disaster was complete. Lisbon was utterly destroyed.

There have been other earthquakes of disastrous proportions recorded in the past several hundred years. We have already mentioned the devastation created by the earthquake in Assam in 1897. No part of the world, it seems, is free from the threat of earthquake disaster at any time in history. Still, there is nothing on record, to date, of an earthquake that created as much devastation, and in as wide an area, as the great Lisbon earthquake of 1755.

9

The
Twentieth Century

Since the beginning of the twentieth century, the world has experienced at least thirty earthquakes of devastating proportions. There were six earthquakes with magnitudes greater than 8 that occurred in 1906 alone. In Chile, the cities of Valparaiso and Santiago were both destroyed by the 1906 earthquakes. In the United States, it was San Francisco that was destroyed by a quake that year.

San Francisco is built on the San Andreas Fault and is one of the cities of the world that is most vulnerable to earthquakes. San Francisco had already experienced severe quakes in 1864, 1898, and again in 1900. But unfortunately the quakes had not stopped the people of San Francisco from erecting houses and office buildings, among other structures, on land that had been filled in, reclaimed from marshes and other wetland. Apparently they did not know, or did not care to know, that anything built on such land was not likely to withstand the shocks from a severe earthquake.

It happened at 5:13 the morning of April 18, 1906. The San Andreas Fault, the greatest fracture in the California crust, suddenly and with no warning shifted, heaved, and rocked the ground on which San Francisco was built.

Immediately and everywhere in the city, walls cracked and buildings crumbled and came down in rubble. Streets buckled and split. Water mains cracked, twisted, and broke. Gas mains ruptured, and gas gushed out in streams to ignite and feed fires in every direction.

The United States government quickly sent soldiers to help the San Francisco firemen and police fight the fires that raged in the city. They were forced to use dynamite and even artillery in an effort to check the holocaust, but the fires burned on. The city burned for three full days, as the survivors watched the mighty conflagration from the surrounding hills.

Damage from that quake extended over an area 450 miles (720 km) long and 50 miles (80 km) wide. Forty-five square miles (117 sq km) of the central part of San Francisco were destroyed. Five hundred and twelve blocks and 28,000 buildings were reduced to rubble. Two hundred and fifty thousand people were forced into the streets, the Presidio, and Golden Gate Park, homeless.

It is rather amazing that the death toll in that quake was not greater than the estimated 700. The property damage ran to an estimated $300 million.

San Francisco, incidentally, is the only city in the United States that has ever been destroyed by an earthquake.

There were other disastrous quakes in the early 1900s. Some have already been mentioned.

Among others, there was the terrible quake that hit the cities of Messina and Reggio in Italy on December 28, 1908. At about 5:20 in the morning, with most of the cities' inhabi-

Opposite: Howard Street in San Francisco buckles as a result of the 1906 quake. Above: San Francisco, the wrecked Hibernia Bank building on the left, lies in ruins. It is the only U.S. city ever to be completely demolished as the result of an earthquake.

tants still in bed, the earth trembled for some twenty seconds, then stopped. But less than two minutes later, the earth heaved, and in shock after shock, houses were shattered and stone buildings were crumbled. Towns, villages, and ports were completely annihilated. Fires broke out all over the area. The inhabitants who were not crushed to death by the tons of falling debris or burned to death in the fires were swept away and drowned in the tsunami brought on by the earthquake. Eighty-four thousand people lost their lives in that catastrophe.

The Kansu earthquake on the sixteenth of December, 1920, destroyed an area of China 280 miles (448 km) by 95 miles (152 km) and killed 180,000. The Kwanto earthquake of 1923, in Japan, mentioned previously, destroyed one-third of Tokyo and all of Yokohama, taking 143,000 lives. The earthquake at Quetta, India, in 1935, took an estimated 50,000 lives.

It must be noted that the casualty report for nearly every earthquake is an estimated number. No census is taken, and there is usually no accounting for the number of people missing as a result of the quake.

One of the most historic earthquakes occurred in Chile in 1960. Active from May 21 through May 29, it began at 6:02 on the morning of the twenty-first in the coastal town of Concepción. The first tremor shook the entire Arauca peninsula and was felt as far away as Chillan, 60 miles (96 km) inland from the coast.

Church towers, houses, and other buildings constructed of brick and stone shuddered and collapsed. Hundreds of people were crushed to death by falling walls and roofs. Many were killed while they still lay in their beds at home.

The shocks that followed the initial one at Concepción came north and south of the sea town, over a stretch of land almost

850 miles (1,360 km) wide. An area of about 50,000 square miles (130,000 sq km) was hit by some 225 earth tremors. These were not slight aftershocks. Ten of them had a magnitude greater than 7. Three of the tremors had a magnitude of more than 8. Magnitude, as already indicated, is a measure of the force of the earthquake at its epicenter. An earthquake with a magnitude of 8 or more promises catastrophe at its epicenter.

The Chilean earthquakes of 1960 created a number of tsunamis that collected their toll of victims, caused more than a thousand landslides that destroyed whole villages, and sank large areas of land as much as 6 feet (1.8 m) into the ground.

It was in 1960, too, as has already been mentioned, that Agadir in Morocco and Lar in Iran were destroyed by earthquakes, with terrible losses of life. The earthquake in Agadir, it is estimated, killed 12,000 people and injured 12,000 more of the 33,000 people who inhabited the town.

The strongest earthquake experienced in North America in the twentieth century, to the best of our knowledge, occurred in Alaska, 80 miles (128 km) east of Anchorage, on March 27, 1964. That earthquake was so powerful that it raised the floor of the ocean between Kodiak and Montague Islands more than 50 feet (15 m). This was the greatest uplift of land by an earthquake ever recorded.

It is estimated that the energy released by the Alaskan earthquake was the equivalent of 40 million tons (36 million m.t.) of TNT. This would be the equivalent of 2,000 of the atomic bombs dropped on Hiroshima at the end of World War II.

The quake was so powerful that it created a tsunami with waves 50 feet (15 m) high. The waves moved at the phenomenal speed of 450 miles (720 km) per hour and for a distance of 8,400 miles (13,500 km).

Because the area was so sparsely settled, the number of

This earthquake-destroyed street is Fourth Avenue, Anchorage, Alaska. The road section on the left dropped 20 feet (.6 m) below the level of the rest of the street. The quake occurred on March 27, 1964.

deaths in the earthquake was limited to 117. The damage caused by the quake was estimated to be around $750 million.

Though there were a number of major earthquakes in the 1970s, in the year 1976 alone, the world suffered at least four earthquakes of devastating proportions. Five thousand two hundred people were killed in the earthquake that hit Guatemala on the fourth of February. On the twenty-eighth of June, an earthquake in Irian-Jaya, Indonesia, killed an estimated 1,000 people; 3,000 more were reported missing. On the seventeenth of August, an earthquake and tsunami in Mindanao, the Philippine Islands, took a toll of 8,000 lives. The greatest earthquake disaster of the year, however, occurred in China on the twenty-eighth of July, 1976.

Just a few months earlier, on May 29, 1976, the province of Yunan in the People's Republic of China had been hit by two severe quakes. How much damage the quakes inflicted is not known. The People's Republic of China releases little information about its internal disasters. Sensitive seismographs, however, can tell us the time and place of even the slightest movement in the earth's crust. On July 28 and 29 in 1976, the seismographs indicated that two major earthquakes had hit Peking, Tientsin, and Tangshan, all in the northeastern section of China. The shocks of those quakes were so powerful that Alaska, many thousands of miles from the epicenter of the earthquakes, was reported to have bounced up and down one-eighth of an inch (.3 cm) during the quakes. That is quite a bounce for a landmass the size of Alaska.

News about the catastrophe trickled very slowly out of China. It came by way of foreign correspondents and tourists visiting the country at the time.

The damage created by the quakes, according to these unofficial reports, was tremendous. Buildings collapsed everywhere, burying people in their rubble. Streets were torn up, cars and trucks smashed. Railroad lines were torn and twisted. The former prime minister of Australia, Gough Whitlam, reported that the Friendship House in Tientsin had split in two.

The government warned that houses still standing might have been severely weakened by the earthquake shocks, and all were in danger of collapsing. Most of the inhabitants of Peking, it was reported, slept outdoors, in any kind of shelter they could hurriedly build for themselves. An estimated six million people, inhabitants of the three cities and the surrounding region, whose houses had already collapsed or were threatening to collapse, made temporary shelters for themselves in the streets and in the fields. Torrential rains that followed the earthquakes did nothing to ease the terrible situation. Aid offered by other countries around the world, in the form of food and medicine for earthquake victims, was refused by the Chinese government.

The People's Republic of China never released any figures on the human casualties of the earthquake nor on the property damage that had occurred. According to unofficial reports, however, the devastation and suffering were extraordinary. As many as 750,000 people might have been killed in the quakes.

There were other powerful earthquakes in the last years of the 1970s. On March 3, 1977, most of the downtown section of Bucharest, Rumania, was destroyed by an earthquake that killed 1,541 and left another 11,275 injured. On September 16, 1978, the city of Tabas in eastern Iran was completely destroyed in a quake that claimed an estimated 25,000 lives.

The earthquake that hit the remote eastern region of Iran

The recent earthquake in southern Italy (November 23, 1980) took at least 5,000 lives.

−56

on January 16, 1979, killing about 200 people and destroying thousands of homes and other buildings, has already been mentioned. The tremendous earthquake that struck the Adriatic shore of Yugoslavia on April 15, 1979, has been treated with some detail in the first chapter of this book.

An earthquake hit northern Kentucky on July 28, 1980. Fortunately, there were no fatalities or injuries. But the quake was strong enough to be felt in fourteen states, from New York and Pennsylvania to Michigan and Wisconsin.

In contrast, the earthquakes that hit Algeria and Italy in late 1980 were utterly devastating. The Algerian quake of October 10, 1980, was centered in Al-Asnam, where an earthquake in 1954 had killed 1,250 people. This time at least 20,000 people were killed. It took only thirty seconds for the quake to destroy almost the entire city.

On November 23, 1980, an earthquake along the Apennine Mountains in southern Italy claimed about 5,000 lives and left about 200,000 people homeless. In Sant' Angelo de Lombardi, at least 300 people were killed, and 90 percent of the houses were destroyed. In Balvano, the façade of the town's medieval church crumbled, killing about 100 people who were attending the Sunday evening mass. The town of Pescopagano was leveled. The center of historic Potenza was reduced to ruins. The story was the same in almost every Italian village over an area of 10,000 square miles (26,000 sq km), including parts of the provinces of Naples (30 miles or 48 km from Eboli, the epicenter of the quake), Avellino, Salerno, and Potenza.

It has been predicted that another major earthquake will hit Chile in the near future, perhaps in 1981. It has also been predicted that the San Andreas Fault will move again within the next fifty years. San Francisco, Los Angeles, and a host of other, smaller cities are built directly on that fault. A major movement of the earth in this area promises nothing less than catastrophe.

10

To Prevent Disaster

There is nothing in nature that creates more havoc and is more devastating than earthquakes. For unmeasured time they have come without any apparent warning, destroying villages, towns, and cities, and taking a dreadful toll of lives.

Many years ago, earthquakes were seen as messages from the gods, who were expressing their anger or delivering punishment for some evil, real or imagined, committed by mere mortals. It was only some 2,500 years ago, with the development of the scientific mind, that people began to think of earthquakes as a phenomenon of nature.

It was some 1,850 years ago, it will be recalled, that Chang Heng, the Chinese astronomer, developed the first instrument to record earthquakes. Modern seismologists and geologists, however, are interested in more than just recording the phenomenon. They are working to discover the causes of earthquakes, ways to predict them, and maybe even ways to prevent them.

It was discovered in this century, for example, that the earth wobbles as it spins around on its axis, and that this wobble creates changes in the earth's magnetism. Changes in the earth's magnetism, it is believed by some seismologists, cause the tectonic plates to shift. And it is the shifting of these plates, it is thought, that causes an earthquake.

A slight disturbance detected in the earth's magnetism in Alaska, just about an hour before the mighty Alaskan earthquake of 1964, seemed to support this theory. But there are two reasons why this may not be true. First, magnetic disturbances come often in Alaska. Second, there have been countless earthquakes that seem not to have been triggered by any kind of magnetic disturbance.

Actually, there is no complete agreement among seismologists and geologists as to the cause of earthquakes. Still, there have been important findings in the study of these quakes, findings that have been accepted by most scientists studying the phenomenon.

For example, Japanese scientists studying the contour of the land have been able, with their findings, to predict earthquakes. A marked tilting in the land, evidently, promises earth tremors or earthquakes. Russian scientists, similarly, have been able to predict earthquakes in their own country after discovering similar tilting of the ground.

Russian scientists have also discovered that an increase in the electrical conductivity of the earth's surface rocks precedes an earthquake. In other words, the surface rocks themselves become better conductors of electricity before an earthquake. Though it was only a moderate tremor, an earthquake in the Kamchatka region of Siberia was predicted this way.

An increase of radon in deep well water, it has been learned, precedes earthquakes. Radon is a radioactive gas that comes with the decay of the element radium. Changes in the stress and tension of crustal rocks, the rocks of the earth's surface, also seem to occur before earthquakes. Small tremors, too, those that can be detected only by very sensitive seismographs, seem to be warnings of earthquakes that may prove devastating.

It was purely by accident that American geologists were able to discover that increased water pressure in the area of a fracture in the earth can create earth tremors or earthquakes.

In 1961, the United States Army at Rocky Mount Arsenal, east of Denver, Colorado, drilled a hole through earth and rock some 2.2 miles (3.6 km) deep. The Army's purpose was to pour contaminated waste water into the hole, water that had been polluted by nerve gas and other deadly matter.

They began to pour water into this hole in 1962. Three years later, geologists reported that there had been 710 earthquakes in the area of the well over the three-year period of waste-water disposal.

The geologists reasoned that the water was seeping into the pores of the deep rock and that the water pressure in the rock was causing it to break apart more easily, releasing tensions in the rock. It seems that old and perhaps inactive faults were able, because of the water pressure, to move again, causing the earth tremors.

For the most part, these earth tremors around Denver were too slight to be felt by the city. However, some were strong enough to have the residents of the area complain about them, even talk about suing the Army for damages.

The Army stopped pouring the contaminated water into the well, and soon the quakes grew fewer in number and came with less frequency. The geologists' suggestion that the Army withdraw all the water it had poured into the well, however, was rejected.

At a later date, a similar suggestion was made to a private company. Chevron Oil had been pumping water into wells some 6,600 feet (2,000 m) deep to aid in the pumping of oil out of the ground. They had been doing this for seven years in their oil fields in western Colorado, and with considerable success. But the process was also responsible for some fifteen to twenty earthquakes a week.

This time, the geologists found a willingness to cooperate. At the geologists' request, the oil company agreed to withdraw the water from four of its wells. Immediately, there was a marked decrease in the number of quakes throughout the oil fields. There were almost no tremors at all around the wells from which the water had been withdrawn.

These findings were exciting. A careful study of them, however, in relation to their possible use in the preventing of earthquakes, led to some difficult but interesting questions.

The suggestion that water be poured into wells to create minor tremors, as a safety valve against possible stronger quakes, was not acceptable. There was no guarantee that such a procedure would not produce more powerful earth tremors and perhaps earthquakes of tremendous magnitude.

It was also pointed out that the energy of an earthquake is generally released well below the level of the wells from which water had been withdrawn in Colorado.

More importantly, there was the question of control. It was argued that geologists had too little knowledge in this area of study to conduct such operations with any degree of safety.

Someday, undoubtedly, geologists and seismologists will be able to predict the coming of earthquakes with considerable accuracy. The problem then will be how to evacuate populated areas in times of danger. Nine million people live in Tokyo. Close to a million people live in Los Angeles. Nearly 700,000 live in San Francisco. Each of these cities has experienced major earthquakes. Each is faced with the possibility of an utterly devastating earthquake at almost any time. And little, if anything, has been done in these major cities to prepare for the possible catastrophe.

The hope remains, of course, that someday our scientists will discover a way to lessen the intensity of earthquakes, perhaps divert them to less inhabited areas. It is not likely, however, on this restless and constantly changing planet, that earthquakes will ever be completely checked or controlled.

If we have learned anything of the history of the earth, we know that the most powerful forces are the forces of nature itself. The best we can do is to continue to study these forces and make whatever effort we can to lessen the calamities and catastrophes they so often visit upon us.

Index